ANCIENT EGYPT
REVEALED

Written by
PETER CHRISP

A Dorling Kindersley Book

DK

LONDON, NEW YORK, MUNICH,
MELBOURNE, and DELHI

SENIOR EDITOR CAREY SCOTT
SENIOR ART EDITOR JOANNE CONNOR
PHOTOSHOP ILLUSTRATOR LEE GIBBONS
DESIGN ASSISTANT JOANNE LITTLE
CATEGORY PUBLISHER SUE GRABHAM
ART DIRECTOR GILLIAN ALLEN
PICTURE RESEARCHER JO HADDON
JACKET DESIGNER CHRIS DREW
DTP DESIGNER JILL BUNYAN
PRODUCTION CONTROLLER DULCIE ROWE

First published in Great Britain in 2002
by Dorling Kindersley Limited,
80 Strand, London WC2R ORL

02 03 04 05 10 9 8 7 6 5 4 3 2 1

A CIP catalogue record for this book is
available from the British Library.

ISBN 0-7513-4149-5

Colour reproduction by
Colourscan, Singapore
Printed in China by
Leo Paper Products

See our complete catalogue at
www.dk.com

CONTENTS

BEGINNINGS

Egyptian civilization developed slowly, over thousands of years. Long before the country was united under a pharaoh, there were specialized craftworkers making necklaces of semi-precious stones. Such necklaces are evidence of a society in which people lived in different classes. Workers made expensive necklaces for nobles to wear.

Carnelian, a semi-precious stone

Deshret, or red crown, worn by pharaohs for more than 3,000 years

Harpoon raised to strike. Its cord is the bronze wire coiled in his right hand

INTO THE PAST

FIVE THOUSAND YEARS AGO, the people of Egypt created one of the earliest and most influential of the world's civilizations. They invented writing, and were the first people to record their own history. A calendar, dividing the year into 12 months, and day and night into 24 hours, was created. Large stone buildings – temples and royal tombs – were built for the first time. These achievements are amazing enough. Yet perhaps the most impressive thing about Egyptian civilization was how long it lasted. It continued, with few changes, for around 3,000 years – 1,000 years longer than the Christian era has existed.

BOY KING

Tutankhamen was a pharaoh who ruled Egypt from around 1336 BC until his early death, in 1327 BC. Few people had heard of him until 1922, when his tomb was discovered by an English archaeologist, Howard Carter. The best preserved of any Egyptian tomb, it contained thousands of treasures. One of them is this beautiful gilded statue of the young pharaoh hunting hippos with a harpoon on the River Nile.

FERTILE FLOODS

The Egyptians lived beside a river, the Nile, which cuts its way through the North African desert. The Nile flooded each year, depositing fertile silt and creating a narrow strip where farmers could grow food. For most of their history, the desert alongside the river protected the Egyptians from foreign invaders. This meant that their civilization stayed free from foreign influences.

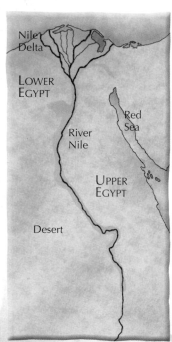

Nile Delta

LOWER EGYPT

Red Sea

River Nile

UPPER EGYPT

Desert

Boat or raft made of wood. In reality, such boats were lashed together with papyrus reeds

HUNTING IN THE AFTERLIFE

The Egyptians believed that, after death, they would live again in another world – the afterlife – which was imagined to be much like Egypt. A lot of our knowledge of daily life actually comes from paintings of the afterlife on tomb walls. People sometimes think that the Egyptians were obsessed with death. Yet paintings like this show how much they loved life. They wanted to carry on living in the same way forever.

Nebamun's wife and daughter accompany him on a hunting trip. This shows how important family life was to the Egyptians

Portrait in the style of Greek and Roman painting

Flowering papyrus plants

Tilapia, a silvery fish still caught in the Nile today

PYRAMIDS OF GIZA

From around 2650 BC until 1800 BC, many Egyptian kings were buried in great stone tombs called pyramids. The biggest of all are those at Giza, built by three kings: Khufu (right), Khafra (centre) and Menkaura (left). In front of Menkaura's pyramid, you can see two smaller pyramids, which he built for his queens. These massive structures have amazed visitors to Egypt ever since they were built, more than four and a half thousand years ago.

Egyptian god Horus

Greek text reads: 'Artimedorus farewell'

MEDITERRANEAN INVASIONS

Egypt was eventually conquered by the Greeks, in 332 BC, and then by the Romans, in 30 BC. Many features of Egyptian life continued under foreign rule, such as the practice of preserving the dead as mummies. This mummy case from soon after AD 100 shows a mixture of Egyptian, Greek, and Roman influences. It belonged to a Greek-speaking Egyptian, called Artimedorus, who appears in the portrait dressed as a Roman.

ROYAL MUMMY

ALMOST THREE YEARS AFTER discovering Tutankhamen's tomb, British archaeologist Howard Carter finally reached the king's mummy. In October 1925, Carter opened the lid of the king's wood and gold coffin. Inside he found another coffin, and inside that, yet another, of solid gold an inch thick. On opening this third coffin, Carter found the mummy, or preserved body, of the dead king. Tutankhamen had been wrapped in linen bandages, which also contained 143 golden amulets and jewels. The king's head was completely covered by a golden portrait mask – the most beautiful work of art that Carter had ever seen.

TINY COFFIN
Carter found two other small coffins in the tomb. This is one of them. Each held the mummified body of a tiny baby girl, possibly Tutankhamen's own babies.

EXPLORING THE MUMMY

1 **Vulture and cobra:** *goddesses of Lower and Upper Egypt*

2 **Gold mask:** *gold was thought of as the flesh of the gods*

3 **Bandages:** *finely woven linen wrapped the king's body*

4 **Blue striped gold headcloth:** *inlaid with coloured glass*

5 **Shrine:** *made from alabaster, holding the king's inner organs*

6 **Skull cap:** *a linen cap decorated with gold and pottery beads*

7 **Inner coffin:** *made from solid gold, one inch thick*

8 **Tiny coffin:** *holding a stillborn baby, also wrapped in bandages*

9 **Vulture pectoral:** *showing Nekhbet, the goddess of Upper Egypt*

10 **Scarabs:** *scarab beetles above lotus flowers on pectoral ornament*

11 **Solar discs:** *held in each of the vulture's talons on pectoral ornament*

12 **Miniature gold coffin:** *holding Tutankhamen's bandaged intestines*

CHEST OF ENTRAILS

This alabaster shrine contained Tutankhamen's canopic jars. These in turn contained miniature coffins that each held one of the king's internal organs.

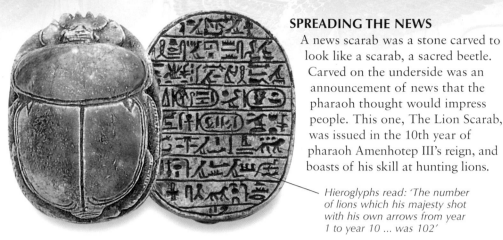

GOD KINGS

To THE EGYPTIANS, their pharaoh, or king, was not just a ruler. He was a god living on earth, and a son of the gods in heaven. In particular, he was linked with Horus, god of the sky, whom he represented while he ruled. The Egyptians believed that the gods had created their world as a place of order and harmony. It was the pharaoh's job to maintain this order.

As chief priest, he spent much of his time performing religious ceremonies while dressed in elaborate royal regalia. The Egyptians were sure that these rites were vital to keep their world working properly. They believed that, thanks to the pharaoh's ceremonies, the sun shone, the crops grew in the fields, and life on earth continued as normal.

Red northern crown

COLOURED CROWNS

Pharaohs wore various crowns, each with its own colour and meaning. The oldest were the tall white *hedjet* and the shorter red *deshret*, which were the crowns of Upper (southern) and Lower (northern) Egypt. In early times, these were two separate kingdoms. Once Egypt was united, in about 3000 BC, pharaohs could wear either crown, or a combination of the two. From about 1550 BC, pharaohs also began to wear a new blue crown, called the *khepresh*.

Experts are unsure whether this bust portrays Hatshepsut or her stepson Tuthmosis

FEMALE PHARAOH

Hatshepsut (above) was one of just six female rulers in Egypt's 3,000-year history. At first, she ruled on behalf of her stepson and nephew, the boy king Tuthmosis III, but soon she made herself pharaoh. Tuthmosis hated his stepmother and, when he eventually became king, he knocked her name off every temple and statue, replacing it with his own.

Blue crown with side ridges, decorated with golden circles

THE STRANGE KING AKHENATEN

Egyptians expected each pharaoh to rule just as
his predecessors had done. So it must have been
a great shock when one pharaoh tried to change
Egypt's religion. His name was Akhenaten, and
he ruled from 1352 to 1336 BC. He banned the
worship of the usual gods, whose images were
destroyed, and tried to get everyone to
worship the Aten, or disc of the sun.

GIFT OF LIFE

The ankh, or life sign,
was a cross with a
loop on top. As well as
being offered by gods to
pharaohs in carvings, it
was made into a powerful
protective amulet. It
was one of the few
Egyptian symbols
that even the poorest
people understood.

FACE TO FACE

Here a pharaoh brings
offerings of wine to the god
Horus. In his right hand,
Horus holds an ankh, the sign
of life, which he will give to
the pharaoh in return. The two
figures are the same size and
stand face to face, showing
their close partnership.

*The Aten sends
down ankhs –
gifts of life*

Statue of King
Akhenaten

SUN WORSHIP

This plaque shows
Akhenaten, his wife Nefertiti
and their daughters, beneath
the life-giving rays of the
Aten. Egyptian gods were
usually worshipped inside
dark temples, but Akhenaten
worshipped his god in the
open air, in temples that
had no roofs.

MARCHING TO WAR

In early times, Egyptian armies always fought on foot. The soldiers were armed with spears, battle axes, clubs, slings, and bows and arrows. These Egyptian foot soldiers, marching off to war, carry large light shields and wooden spears tipped with bronze points.

Shield of animal skin over a wooden frame

WARRIOR NATION

IN WALL CARVINGS ON TEMPLES, pharaohs liked to be pictured as huge and mighty warriors, crushing tiny enemies beneath the wheels of their chariots. Egyptians often saw foreign peoples as a threat to the natural order – the harmony created by the gods when they made the land of Egypt. So, pharaohs were often depicted defeating their enemies to show them preserving order. During early Egyptian history, warfare took the form of expeditions into neighbouring African lands, such as Nubia to the south. One purpose was to conquer and control the rich Nubian gold supply. Later, in the second millennium BC, a series of pharaohs led the Egyptian army into Asia, where they conquered a true empire.

CHARIOTS OF WAR

The horse-drawn chariot was a light, fast vehicle, used as a moving platform for archers. It was introduced to Egypt by people from Palestine, called the Hyksos, who moved into northern Egypt in the middle of the second millennium BC. The Egyptians quickly took to fighting in chariots and used the new weapon to drive the Hyksos out. After defeating them, the Egyptians went on to conquer neighbouring lands in Asia.

Fan bearers run in step, showing the good order of the army

Relief from Tutankhamen's gilded chariot

CAPTIVES

Egyptian art often shows foreigners bound as prisoners of war as a sign of Egypt's superiority. Such prisoners were sometimes forced to become slaves, working in mines and quarries. The bearded man depicted here comes from one of the lands to the northeast of Egypt, while the other pair is Nubian.

The lion-headed Sekhmet with a sun disc behind her head

WRISTBAND

Egyptian noblemen were skilled at archery, which they practised when hunting along the Nile. An archer gripped the bow in his left hand and drew back the string with his right. He wore a guard on his wrist to protect him from the whip of the bowstring when it was released.

WEAPONS

The earliest Egyptian arrowheads were made of razor sharp flint. However, flint takes hours of careful chipping to make just one arrowhead. Bronze arrowheads and spearheads were more practical since they could be mass produced in moulds.

GODDESS OF WAR

The lion-headed Sekhmet was the goddess of aggression. When the Egyptians went to war, they believed that Sekhmet, as well as other gods and goddesses, fought alongside them. Sekhmet was linked with the sun, whose burning destructive power she was believed to turn against the enemies of Egypt.

Scene from the side of a box discovered in Tutankhamen's tomb

Scattered and fleeing Nubians, representing disorder

PERFUMED WIGS

These women wear 'incense cones' made of animal fat mixed with perfume. The fat would melt, scenting their wigs. Some experts believe that these were not worn in real life, and were a way of showing, in art, that wigs and hair were perfumed.

Cone of perfumed fat

Decorative headband

IDEAS OF BEAUTY

THE EGYPTIANS WERE LOVERS OF BEAUTY, and both men and women wanted to look as attractive as possible. People wore kilts and dresses of white linen, which acted as a plain background against which all kinds of colourful jewellery could be displayed. Those who could afford it wore wigs, made from human hair and often scented. Just like today, Egyptian fashions in clothes, hair, and makeup changed over time. Yet, unlike modern fashions, these changes took place slowly and gradually over hundreds of years. This was because the Egyptians believed that their lives had been created by the gods, who knew the perfect way to live. They saw little value in novelty or change for the sake of it.

LUCKY NECKLACE

Men and women wore jewellery both as decoration and for luck, as certain images were believed to protect the wearer against evil. This lovely necklace has a tiny figure of Heh, god of eternity, in the middle. Such a necklace may have been given to someone to wish them a long and safe life.

Heh, god of eternity

Turquoise bead

Lapis lazuli bead

Cowrie shells made from electrum, a mixture of gold and silver

SHOWING STATUS

The Egyptians used hair to display rank and status. Children had their heads shaved except for one long lock – the sidelock of youth. The pharaoh on the right is wearing a false beard attached by a strap, a sign of royalty.

Sidelock of youth

A PRIVATE MOMENT

This king with his queen may represent Tutankhamen and Ankesenamun. They are dressed in the finest pleated linen clothes and wear elaborately jewelled collars and coloured sashes. Both wear royal cobras on their heads. The queen offers lotus flowers, which were appreciated for their strong fragrance, to her husband.

Makeup jar of coloured glass

Malachite

Fish amulet, believed to prevent drowning

False beard, or sidelock, of hair

Galena

Red ochre

COSMETICS

Men as well as women used makeup, which has been found in the tombs of both sexes. They wore eye liner made at first from a green mineral called malachite, and later from galena (lead sulphide), which was deep black. Women painted their lips red with ochre, and also used it as a blusher on their cheeks.

Collar decorated with flowers

Almost transparent linen dress

BEAUTIFUL LADY

Queen Nefertiti was the chief wife of Pharaoh Akhenaten. Her name means 'The Beautiful Lady is Come'. The discovery in 1912 of this painted limestone bust showed that Nefertiti lived up to her name. She wears a tall blue crown, which was unique to her. Beneath the crown, Nefertiti's head is shaved, drawing attention to her long, elegant neck. This is one of the most famous works of Egyptian art, still constantly reproduced and sold to tourists as a souvenir.

LIFE ON THE NILE

FOR THOUSANDS OF YEARS, Egyptian boats travelled up and down the River Nile. They sailed or rowed upriver, against the fast-flowing currents. To travel back down, the sails were lowered and the boats carried by the current. This crew have almost finished loading their boat. Both crew and boat belong to the god Thoth and his temple at the city of Khnum. The crew have travelled to the temple's farming estates, collecting goods for the god and the priests who serve him in his temple. Their most important passenger is a baboon, sacred to Thoth, who has come all the way from Punt, far to the southeast.

EXPLORING LIFE ON THE NILE

1 **Sacred baboon:** *perched on the rigging – to be cared for at the temple*

2 **Hull:** *made of wood from the acacia tree*

3 **Rigging:** *for raising a single sail made from linen*

4 **Ibis:** *the wading bird, which, like the baboon, was sacred to Thoth*

5 **Produce:** *terracotta jugs of wine and barrels of fruit*

6 **Live goats:** *fresh meat for the priests in the temple*

7 **Goods:** *sacks of wheat and barley for making bread and beer*

8 **Handheld steering oars:** *one on each side of the boat*

9 **Hippopotamuses:** *sometimes hunted by rich Egyptians*

10 **Crocodile:** *the most dangerous animal in the River Nile*

THE NILE

It hardly ever rains in Egypt. In ancient times, farming was only possible around the banks of the Nile, which flooded every year, swollen by spring rains far to the south. When the flood went down, it left behind rich black silt, ideal for growing crops. The Egyptians called their country *Kemet*, meaning the 'black land', after this silt. Beyond the black land, there was the red land of the desert, where nothing could grow.

DAILY LIFE

MOST EGYPTIANS were poor peasant farmers who worked the land, often on great estates owned by the pharaoh and the temples. Farm work began in the autumn when the Nile floods went down. The farmers broke up the soil with hoes and ploughs pulled by oxen. Then they scattered seeds, which were trodden into the earth by sheep, goats, and pigs. In the spring, they harvested their crops by hand. Although Egyptian peasants worked hard, their lives were easier than those of many ancient farmers. They did not need to add fertilizers to their fields, since the Nile flood gave them new soil every year. They also had a break from farm work for almost three months when the land was covered by the floodwaters.

Axe blade

WOODWORK

Today, there are few trees in Egypt other than palm trees, which are of limited use in woodworking. In ancient times, acacias and sycamores grew along the Nile and these were used to make river boats, furniture, and the handles of tools like these. Cedar wood was imported from the Lebanon to make seafaring boats and coffins.

Adze for planing wood

Blade of axe made from bronze

Hoe with a blade of sharpened wood

VITAL TOOL

One letter in the Egyptian alphabet, the sound 'mr', was a drawing of a hoe. This was the Egyptian farmer's most important tool. It was made from two pieces of wood tied together with plant fibre rope. Farmers used hoes to break up the soil before planting and for weeding the growing crops.

WINEMAKING

Grapes grow well in the warm climate of northern Egypt. These workers are collecting the fruit, to be made into wine. The grapes were placed in large vats, where men crushed them with their feet to extract the juice. Wine was also made from dates, figs, and pomegranates. Only richer Egyptians drank wine, but beer, which was brewed from barley, was enjoyed by everyone.

GRINDING GRAIN

This woman is grinding wheat into flour, using two stones called a 'saddle quern'. The flour was used to make bread, the basic food of every Egyptian. She pushes the smaller stone backwards and forwards on the grain, which rests on the long lower curved stone. Saddle querns were invented about nine thousand years ago and are still used in parts of Africa today.

Women worked alongside their husbands in the fields

Curved sickle with little flint blades

GATHERING THE HARVEST

This harvesting scene comes from the tomb of a man called Sennedjem. He and his wife, Iyeneferti, are shown gathering the harvest in the afterlife. This shows just how important farming was to ancient Egyptians. They believed that there would always be farm work to be done, even after death.

Scribes recording the size of the grain harvest

A scribe's equipment included pen and ink box, papyrus roll, and a water pot

Workers portrayed as smaller than scribes, showing their lesser importance

KEEPING STOCK

Scribes were much like local government officers today. Under instructions from Egypt's rulers, they made accounts of the size of the harvests, calculated taxes, and prepared orders for temples and army supplies throughout the kingdom. Scribes were probably even more important than the pharaoh's armies in making Egypt a united kingdom.

THE WRITTEN WORD

THE EGYPTIANS WERE probably the first people to invent writing, some time before 3,000 BC. They wrote using picture signs that represented words, ideas, or sounds. For most of Egyptian history, there were two styles of writing. Hieroglyphs (holy carvings) were the picture signs used on wall carvings and paintings. Hieratic (priestly) was a hieroglyphic shorthand, invented for writing quickly. There were dozens of uses for writing: Egyptians wrote books on subjects such as medicine and mathematics; they wrote business and personal letters, stories, and government records. They also wrote spells on tomb walls. To the Egyptians, writing had great magical power. It was called *medu-neter*, meaning 'the words of the gods'.

GOD OF WRITING

Like everything else in Egypt, writing had its own god. Thoth, also the god of knowledge, the moon, and time, was believed to have invented writing. He had the head of a river bird, or ibis, though he was sometimes shown as a baboon, too. Four pharaohs were named after him. They were called Tuthmosis, which means 'born of Thoth'.

A RESPECTABLE PROFESSION

Egyptians who were trained to read and write are called 'scribes', from the Latin word 'scribere', meaning to write. They were so highly respected for their knowledge that sculptures of Egyptian nobles often show them as scribes, even if they were not! This scribe sits cross-legged, writing on a roll of papyrus resting on his tightly stretched kilt. Holding the roll in his left hand, he writes from right to left. The fat on his belly shows that he does not do physical work.

LEARNING TO WRITE

The English alphabet has only 26 letters, but young Egyptian scribes had to learn more than 1,000 signs before they could read and write. We do not know how many Egyptians could write, but it is likely that the number was very small, and that it included very few women. Schools were open only to boys.

Pottery relief showing students practising writing

Hieroglyphs were written in columns

PENS AND INK

Scribes originally used pens made from reeds by chewing the ends to form a brush. Pointed pens, like these shown to the left, were also made from reeds, but the reed was split to hold the ink inside. The black ink was a solid cake, made from soot or charcoal mixed with gum. The scribe dipped his pen in his water pot and then rubbed it on the ink.

Cake of black ink

A scribe's pens and ink in a wooden box

WRITING ON PAPER

This papyrus sheet shows the two main styles of writing; hieratic and hieroglyphs. The hieroglyphs appear above the picture of a high priest making an offering to the god Osiris, and on the left the script is in hieratic. Egyptian paper was made from the inner core of papyrus plants, which grew in the marshes of the Nile.

Hieratic script was written right to left

Four hieroglyphic symbols make up the name Nebkheperura

WHAT'S IN A NAME?

Pharoahs wore gold rings, on which their names and titles were written in hieroglyphs. They used them as seals, pressing them into wax to sign letters and documents. This ring, which belonged to Tutankhamen, spells out the name he adopted when he became king: *Nebkheperura*, which means 'Ra is Lord of Becomings'.

MAKING BEADS

In this tomb painting, one jeweller makes stone beads while a second sews them onto a broad collar. The man in front is using a bow to make holes in the beads. He has passed its string around three bronze drills. By quickly moving his bow backwards and forwards, he sets the drills spinning.

CRAFTSMANSHIP

EGYPTIAN CRAFTSMEN worked in large workshops, which were often owned by the pharaoh or the great temples. They were highly skilled in many different crafts, including glass-making, stone carving, gold working, and pottery. Using tools made of stone, bronze, and copper, they were able to cut and shape the hardest stones to make beads and other ornaments. We know a lot about the craft workers of Egypt because Egyptians placed everyday items, as well as their most treasured possessions, in tombs. Thanks to the dry desert air, these items have been preserved for thousands of years. Tombs also contain wall paintings showing busy craftsmen at their work.

MUMMY CASES

Gold was very expensive. For large objects, such as mummy cases, it was usually only used as gilding. This case was carved from wood, and then covered with a thin skin of gold. Another popular and cheap material for mummy cases was 'cartonnage' — layers of linen stiffened with plaster and shaped into the human form. Cartonnage mummy cases could also be gilded.

POTTERY PRODUCTION

The Egyptians discovered various ways of making bowls and pots. One clever method involved using finely ground quartz sand mixed with lime, ash or salt, and water. The mixture, called faience, could be worked by hand or pushed into a pottery mould to mass-produce pots. These faience vessels both use a favourite Egyptian decoration, lotus flowers.

FLESH OF THE GODS

Gold, which is scarce, bright, and never rusts, has always been the most highly prized metal. The Egyptians were lucky to have a gold supply, which made them the envy of all their neighbours. It was mined in the eastern desert, and also brought from Nubia, to the south. People described gold as the flesh of the gods, and often used this gleaming metal to make goods for the royal dead. Its softness made it useless for tools, but meant that it could be easily worked by craftsmen, making beautiful ormanents, such as this pectoral collar, from the tomb of Tutankhamen.

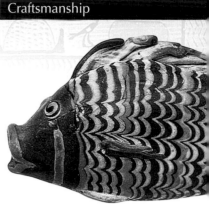

GLASS EXPERTS

To make this colourful fish-shaped perfume container, Egyptian glass-makers fixed a core of sand and mud to a metal rod and dipped it in molten glass. This was then shaped by rolling on a stone. Stripes were added by winding thin rods of different coloured glass around it.

Head of Horus suggests that the harp was used in religious ceremonies

Pipe

Lute

Harp with 13 strings

Animal gut strings

Royal cobra with the wings of a vulture

Tuning pegs to tighten the strings

MUSICAL INSTRUMENTS

The Egyptians loved music, which was played during festivals, religious ceremonies, and at dinner parties. Craftsmen made many types of instruments, including pipes, cymbals, trumpets, harps, and lutes. This wooden harp with animal gut strings is more than 3,000 years old, and yet it could still be played today.

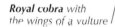

Head of pharaoh

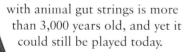

Women musicians play at a funeral banquet

Hollow wooden sound box gave volume to the vibrating strings

TEMPLE SECRETS

CARVED FROM SOLID ROCK, the great
temple at Abu Simbel was built
more than three thousand years
ago. It is dedicated to three gods –
Amun-Ra, Ra-Horakhty, and Ptah.
The temple's builder was Pharaoh
Rameses II, whose colossal statues
sit outside in the bright sunlight
and line the dark entrance hall.
Just twice each year, at dawn,
the sun's rays penetrate the
temple, bathing the statues of
Rameses and two of the gods
in their light. Why Ptah was
placed to stay in shadow is a
mystery. Today, thousands
of tourists visit Abu Simbel
each year. But, in Egyptian
times, the temple was the
home of the gods and the
workplace of the priests
who were their servants.

EXPLORING THE TEMPLE

1   **Queen Nefertari:** *statue of Pharaoh Rameses II's wife*

2   **Pharaoh's foot:** *20-metre-high statue damaged by earthquake in 27 BC*

3   **Shaven-headed priest:** *has brought offerings to the gods*

4   **Gods:** *from left to right: Ptah, creator god (in shadow); Amun, king of the gods; Pharaoh Rameses II, worshipped here alongside the gods; and Ra-Horakhty, god of the sun*

5   **Offering table:** *strewn with food and flowers – gifts to the gods*

6   **Sunbeam:** *illuminates Rameses and the gods Ra-Horakhty and Amun*

7   **Wall paintings:** *showing Rameses bringing offerings*

8   **Rameses II:** *name written on his upper arm*

DIVINE PHARAOH
At Abu Simbel, Rameses II was worshipped along with the gods. This was unusual because, though pharaohs were thought of as the sons of gods, they were not usually worshipped as fully divine until after their deaths. In the 1960s, the Great Temple was threatened with flooding, and was taken apart and reassembled on higher ground.

RAM LIONS
Every year, at the temple of Amun-Ra at Karnak, priests took the cult statue of the god Amun-Ra across the Nile to visit the dead pharaohs. Mythical beasts called criosphinxes guard the processional way. Each criosphinx has the body of a lion and the head of a ram.

TEMPLE WORSHIP

AN EGYPTIAN TEMPLE was seen as the home of a god, who was believed to have real physical needs like a human being. Every morning, the priests went into the sanctuary, where the god's statue was kept inside a bolted wooden shrine. After opening the shrine, they kissed the ground as a mark of respect. They brought the statue out, undressed it, and washed it with water from the temple's sacred lake. Each day, the statue was given a new set of clothes and fresh makeup, and offered a meal from the food on the table of offerings. During religious festivals, the priests carried the god outside the temple in a procession.

The priest brings a duck as a food offering to feed the soul of the dead pharaoh

HOLY WATER
Temples had a sacred lake whose water was used for purification — ritual cleaning. As well as washing themselves twice each day and twice at night, the priests washed the gods, and poured water over temple offerings. This bronze vessel, a situla, was used to pour the water.

SERVANTS OF THE GODS
A leopard skin identifies this man as a 'sem' priest — a chief priest in charge of a funerary temple. There were many different types of priest with different ranks. Some had special knowledge, such as those who scheduled the religious festivals. Others simply swept the temples. The Egyptian name for priest was *hem neter*, meaning god's servant.

Tapered base for resting on a stand

SACRED RATTLE

This sistrum, a sort of rattle, was shaken by women during ceremonies for Hathor, the goddess of beauty, joy, and music. Her sacred animal was the cow. The head of Hathor on the sistrum's handle has cow's ears.

MUSIC AND DANCE

Women played an important role in temple worship as dancers, singers, and musicians. The pharaoh himself sometimes joined in their dances. A hymn to the goddess Hathor, the wife of Horus, written on her temple walls, declares: 'The pharaoh comes to dance and sing! Mistress, see the dancing! Wife of Horus, see the skipping!'

Dance was one form of temple worship

Cow's horns indicate that this is Hathor

A MEAL FOR THE GODS

Every temple had a Hall of Offerings, where tables were piled high with food, brought as daily meals for the gods and goddesses. In return for their food, the gods gave life. This is symbolized by the ankh — the sign for life, held by goddess Hathor. The woman on the right is Queen Nefertari, wife of Rameses II. She brings wine to Hathor, who is shown in her human form. After the food had been offered to the gods, it was taken away and eaten by the priests.

Cup containing wine

Table of offerings for the gods and goddesses

Ankh, the symbol for life

HOUSEHOLD GOD

This funny-looking god called Bes was one of the few not linked with an animal. He is generally shown sticking out his tongue to scare away evil spirits. Bes was popular with ordinary people, who kept statues like this in their homes. He was a protector who drove away evil spirits, poisonous snakes, and scorpions.

The vulture's outstretched wings showed it was a protector

ANIMAL GODS

Horus wears the pharaoh's double crown

EVERY ANCIENT EGYPTIAN BELIEVED in many different gods, who were thought to watch over everything that happened on earth and in the afterlife. Gods made the sun rise in the morning, and gave life to people, animals, and plants. Different gods had different roles. Their powers and characteristics, such as strength, speed, or protectiveness, were like those of the animals and birds that lived in Egypt. So most of the gods were represented by the animals whose characteristics they shared. There were hundreds of gods, and it is easy to get confused by them. One god could appear in different forms, as a human, an animal, or a mixture of the two. To add to the confusion, over time gods often took on each other's features and roles.

Horus and Seth tie a northern papyrus to a southern lotus plant, uniting Lower and Upper Egypt

GOD OF CHAOS

Seth was the god of disorder and confusion and enemy of Horus, the hawk-headed god of the sky. Seth was thought to have murdered his brother, Osiris, who was Horus's father. Although rivals, they were also sometimes seen as partners. This carving shows Horus and Seth uniting the kingdoms of Upper and Lower Egypt.

HORUS THE HAWK

The hawk-headed Horus was the god of kingship and the special protector of the pharaoh. His name means 'he who is far above'. It is easy to see why the Egyptians chose a hawk for this role – among the birds, the hawk looks like a king. Each pharaoh was thought to be the embodiment of Horus, and was called the 'living Horus'.

The atef, a
feathered
crown

SUN WORSHIP

Ra, the sun god, is a good example of a god who took several different forms. In the daytime, he had the head of a hawk with a sun disc on top. Here, you can see the form he took during the night as he travelled through the underworld. He has the head of a ram and the body and wings of a vulture.

Ra holds amulets in his claws

CROCODILE GOD

Here, Sobek, a crocodile god, wears ram's horns, cobras, and a sun disc – all features of other gods. Sobek's worshippers did this to show that he was more powerful than these other gods because he had taken on all their strengths.

KHNUM THE MAKER

This ram-headed god was called Khnum. He was a potter who made the first people out of clay, and also shaped every baby before it was born. He was especially worshipped in the far south of Egypt, where he watched over the source of the River Nile.

PROTECTING THE DEAD

As well as watching over the living, gods were believed to protect the dead. The gods in this painting stand guard in front of a tomb. On the right are two goddesses of birth, Opet and Hathor. They are there to help the dead person be reborn into a new life. The hawk-headed god on the left is Sokar, one form of Osiris, ruler of the dead.

Osiris-Sokar, wrapped in bandages like a mummy

Hathor, the cow goddess

Opet, a hippo with a crocodile tail

ROYAL TOMB

BRITISH ARCHAEOLOGIST Howard Carter began searching the Valley of the Kings for Tutankhamen's tomb in 1917. In November, 1922, he discovered a stairway, the entrance to the lost tomb. A few weeks later, Carter, his sponsor Lord Carnarvon, Carnarvon's daughter Lady Evelyn, and Carter's friend Arthur Callendar stood in a dark corridor, in front of a sealed doorway. Carter knocked a hole in the wall and pushed in his candle. What he saw was so astonishing, he was speechless. Unable to bear the tension, Carnarvon asked, 'Can you see anything?' 'Yes', Carter gasped, 'Wonderful things!'

On top of this box lay a beautiful faience broad collar, and a set of faience rings threaded onto a strip of linen

TREASURE BOX
This simple box contained pieces of a jewelled corslet, decorated with figures of Tutankhamen and the gods, including Amun-Ra. It would take Carter years to open and inspect all the boxes. Every item had to be photographed and carefully recorded.

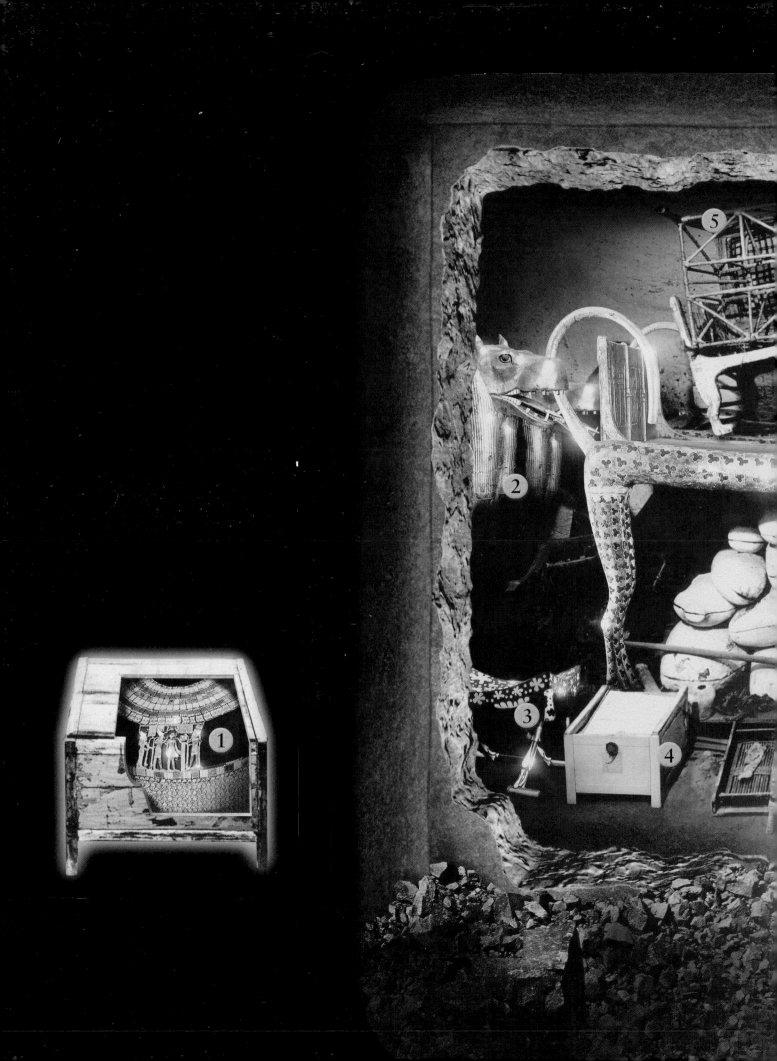

EXPLORING THE TOMB

1   **Corslet:** *gold, semiprecious stones, and colored glass*

2   **Ammut:** *decoration on a bed showing Ammut, eater of the dead*

3   **Cross-legged stool:** *carved ebony wood decorated with ivory inlay*

4   **White-washed box:** *originally contained the king's shaving equipment*

5   **Chair:** *made from ebony wood and papyrus*

6   **Wooden bed:** *simple white-washed bed with woven linen mattress*

7   **Royal bed:** *tail of a third bed, decorated as a lioness*

8   **Bow-fronted traveling box:** *decorated with strips of wood and gold inlay*

9   **Ritual couch:** *gilded wood & blue glass, in a form of the cow goddess, Hathor*

10   **White boxes:** *containing joints of meat for the king to eat in the afterlife*

BURIAL CHAMBER

To the right of the first room, Carter found the royal burial chamber. It contained four gilded shrines. This door, decorated with the goddess Isis, comes from the third shrine. Tutankhamen lay inside the shrines, in his set of four coffins.

VALLEY OF THE KINGS

During the New Kingdom period (1550–1069 BC), pharaohs, nobles, and tomb makers were buried in rock-cut tombs, in the desert to the west of the city of Thebes. The west, where the sun sets, has always been linked with death. Nothing grows in the desert, so time seems to stand still there. This made it the perfect site for tombs.

Ancient path made by the tomb makers

Tomb entrance

BUILDING TOMBS

The sphinx faces east towards the rising sun

ONE OF THE FIRST ACTS of a new pharaoh was to give orders for the building of his tomb. Pharaohs took more care over their tombs than they did over their palaces. Pharaoh Khafra's palace, made of mud-brick, crumbled to dust thousands of years ago. Yet his vast stone pyramid still stands in the Egyptian desert, guarded by a mighty sphinx, 20 metres (65 ft) high and 73 metres (237 ft) long. To us, it seems odd to lavish such care on the dead. Yet it made perfect sense to Pharaoh Khafra. He knew that he would only live on earth for a short time, so he did not need to waste his time building a palace made of stone. His tomb, however, would be his home for all eternity.

RESTING PLACE

Khafra's sarcophagus (stone coffin) lies protected in a chamber at the heart of the pyramid.

For most of its history, the sphinx has been covered to the neck in the shifting desert sands

KING'S HEAD

This great sphinx at Giza was the earliest large-scale sculpture made by the Egyptians. Khafra was able to build this, and the pyramid behind, because he ruled Egypt for such a long time. His reign lasted 26 years, from 2558 to 2532 BC. The head is that of the king himself, wearing a striped royal head-cloth, called a nemes. The body is a lion, the king of the animals. So the sphinx probably represents Khafra's royal power.

GOODS FOR THE DEAD

Pharaohs and rich nobles were buried with everything they would need to live in luxury in the afterlife. These men are carrying furniture to the tomb of Ramose, an important nobleman in the time of Amenhotep III, and his son Akhenaten. Egyptian tombs were often decorated with paintings like this. The Egyptians believed that the paintings would magically come to life when the items in them were needed by the dead person.

TOMB INTERIOR

This tomb belonged to a man called Pashedu, a workman from Deir el-Medina, a tomb workers' village close to the Valley of the Kings. Pashedu himself is the figure kneeling beneath the palm tree.

Gold corslet

Eyes of Horus to protect the mummy

MUMMY CASES

The rich were often placed inside a set of mummy cases, one inside the other. The cases were taken to the tomb by priests, who used a boat to cross the Nile, and then dragged the coffin on a sledge. The cases acted as both a home and, most importantly, a substitute body for the dead person.

Mummy cases of a priestess who served the god Amun-Ra

STANDING GUARD

Every pharaoh's tomb would have been magically guarded by statues. This statue of Tutankhamen is one of a pair who stood guard outside the sealed door of his burial chamber. Despite such guards, all the royal tombs, except Tutankhamen's, were robbed of all their treasures during ancient Egyptian times.

Wood covered with black resin

Female
mummy
preserved
some time
after 600 BC

MUMMY MAKER
Mummification had its own special
god, Anubis, who had the head of a
black jackal (wild dog). This tomb
painting shows Anubis
working on the mummy
of a man called
Sennedjem. One of
the priests overseeing
the mummification
process wore the mask
of Anubis, acting the
role of the god.

MUMMIFICATION

Egyptians believed that it was possible to live again
after death, but only if the body was preserved. If the
body was destroyed, the dead person's soul would have
nowhere to live. So every Egyptian who could afford it had
his or her body preserved – turned into a mummy. First the
soft organs were removed. The body was then packed inside
and out with natron, a salty substance, and left to dry out for
40 days. After being washed, stuffed,
and rubbed with oils and resins, it was
wrapped in linen bandages. Magic
charms, called amulets, were placed in
the bandages, to protect the mummy
and help it to come back to life again.

*Wax plate, decorated with the
eye of Horus, was placed over
the cut in the corpse's flesh*

WITHIN THE WRAPPINGS
On this unwrapped mummy, you can
see a cut made on the left side. The
inner organs were removed, and the
body stuffed with linen or sawdust,
through this opening. Only the
heart and the kidneys were left
inside. The Egyptians thought
that the heart was the seat of
the personality – the place
where we feel emotions and
think. The kidneys were
just too difficult to reach.

*Body coated head-
to-toe in resin to
preserve it*

Ritual
knife

Tool used
to whisk
the brain

BRAIN DRAIN
Oddly enough,
while the heart, liver,
intestines, stomach, and
lungs were all carefully
preserved, the brain was
thrown away. The Egyptians
did not know that the brain
was an important organ. They
would push a hooked blade up
through the nostrils, and whisk the
brain until it turned to liquid. It was
then drained out through the nose.

Female mummy, well-protected by amulets

OPEN WIDE

The most important part of a funeral was called the 'opening of the mouth', carried out in front of the dead person's tomb. While one priest held the mummy upright, others would tap it on the mouth with special tools. This was believed to restore the dead person's speech, sight, and hearing.

Female mourners

Horus, powerful protector against evil

Heart scarab, protecting the dead person

LUCKY CHARMS

Magic charms, called amulets, were placed in the bandages to protect the mummy and to bring it good luck. Each amulet had its own special meaning. This one shows one of the winged goddesses who protected the dead, either Isis or Nepthys. She stretches out her wings protectively over a scarab, a sign of the dead person's rebirth and self-renewal.

Anubis guards the mummy, armed with a flail (whip)

Duamutef, god of the dead person's stomach

Shabti figure to help in the next world

CANOPIC JARS

The dead person's liver, stomach, intestines, and lungs were separately preserved. Each was wrapped in bandages and stored in its own 'canopic jar', protected by a god, whose head often appeared as the stopper. Shown on the right are the baboon-headed Hapy (lungs) and the jackal-headed Duamutef (stomach), both sons of Horus. The jars were put in a chest and placed in the tomb, near the mummy.

Jar for the lungs

Jar for the stomach

DEATH OF A NOBLE

This man, setting off on his journey into the afterlife, is an Egyptian noble. Usually, only the rich could afford to have an elaborately painted tomb, or be buried with their own guide to the underworld (a Book of the Dead). We cannot know for certain how poorer Egyptians saw death, but it is likely that they too believed that they would live again, even without this help.

THE AFTERLIFE

FOR THE EGYPTIANS, death was the start of a long and dangerous journey. Before reaching the afterlife, the dead person would have to travel through a dark underworld, avoiding monsters, poisonous snakes, and lakes of fire. Guidebooks for the journey were written on papyrus rolls and painted on mummy cases and on tomb walls. These 'Books of the Dead' listed the dangers that the dead would encounter, and the magic spells that would protect them. Each book was specially painted for an individual, who was shown facing the perils of the underworld before being reborn.

Professional mourners from a wall-painting in the tomb of an important official, Ramose

Loose hair was a sign of mourning

WEEPING WOMEN

Even though the Egyptians believed that they would live again after death, they still mourned the dead with great sorrow. Female mourners watched the funeral procession pass by, on its way to the tomb. They showed their grief by wailing, raising their arms in the air, and scattering dirt on their heads.

Khepri, god of rebirth and the sun's journey

Dead person being taken to the afterlife

INTO THE UNDERWORLD

Living by the River Nile, it was natural for the Egyptians to think of the journey to the afterlife as one made by boat. Every night, when the sun set in the west, it was believed to descend into the underworld, through which it had to travel before being reborn in the east at dawn. The dead also had to sail through a dark underworld, called the Amduat, before being reborn in the afterlife. In this wall painting, the dead man travels in the boat of the sun.

WEIGHING THE HEART

The dead had to pass a test called 'the weighing of the heart'. Watched over by Anubis, protector of the dead, the heart was weighed on a scale against the feather of Maat, goddess of truth and justice. If the heart was lighter than the feather, it meant that the person had lived a good life. If the heart was too heavy, it would be gobbled up by Ammut, the 'eater of the dead'.

Ostrich feather of Maat

Thoth records the result of the test

Horus leads Ani, the dead man, to Osiris

Heart

Anubis checks the balance

Ammut

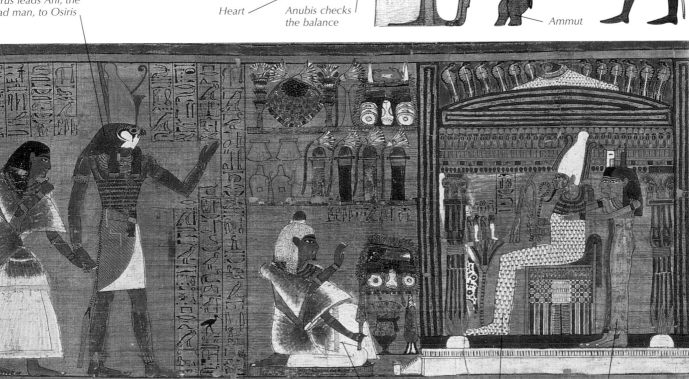

MEETING OSIRIS

Once the dead person had passed the weighing of the heart test, he was led by Horus to meet Osiris, king and judge of the dead. This papyrus shows Horus introducing a man called Ani to Osiris. Horus is saying, 'I have brought Ani to you. His heart has been weighed by Thoth and found to be just.' Ani then kneels and makes offerings to Osiris, asking the king to allow him to live in his kingdom.

Ani, his wig now white, presents offerings to Osiris

Osiris, shown with green skin, which stands for new life

Isis and Nepthys, sisters of Osiris. Isis was also his wife

Thoth, god of writing and author of the Books of the Dead, acts as guide

BIRD SOUL

The Egyptians believed that every person had two souls, called the *ka* and the *ba*. The ka was the life-force, while the ba was the personality and the power to move. In order for the dead to survive in the afterlife, their *bas* had to make a nightly journey between their physical bodies, preserved in the tombs, and the underworld.

The ba is shown as a bird with a human head

INDEX

ACKNOWLEDGEMENTS

Dorling Kindersley would like to thank:
Clare Lister, Sarah Goulding, and Edda Bohnsack for editorial assistance. Adrienne Hutchinson, Ann Cannings and Vicky Wharton for design assistance. Charlotte Oster for DK picture research, Dorothy Frame for the index.

The publisher would like to thank the following for their kind permission to reproduce their photographs:
Key: a=above b=bottom c=centre l=left r=right t=top
AKG London: 11clb, 14-15bc, 18-19, 20-21, 22-23, 26bl, 27bc; Egyptian Museum, Cairo Acetate 8b; Francois Guenet 26-27tc, 33tc; Eric Lessing 9br, 18cb, 19ca, 21br, 23cb, 32tl, 34tc;

Robert O'Dea 3crb, 26tr. **Ancient Art & Architecture Collection:** 9ca, 9bc, 23tc, 35tr; Bob Partridge 8bl; R Sheridan 6c; Acetate 9 crb. **The Ancient Egypt Picture Library:** Bob Partridge 1tc/bc, 2-3, 10-11, 12-13, 14-15, Acetate 31, 32-33, 32cr, 34-35, 36-37, 38tc/bc; 37tr. **Ardea London Ltd:** 3tr, 3cl, 7t, 20cl. **Bolton Metro:** 2. **Bridgeman Art Library, London/New York:** 1c, 10br, 19bc, 30clb, 31clb, 36cra; Ashmolean Museum, Oxford, 26-27; 28-29; British Museum 37c; British Museum/Mrs Nina de Garis Davies, 20cla; Egyptian National Museum, Cairo Acetate 31, Acetate 8 br, 9br, 9-9cb, 11tr, 12cr, 12bl, 13bc, Acetate 31, 33br; Illustrated London News Picture Library, London Acetate 30crb; Louvre, Paris 20br, 36tl;

36-37bc; Museo Archeologico, Florence 21ca. **British Museum:** 3bl, 6tl, 7br, Acetate 8cla 10tl, 10tl, 10tr, 11ca, 13c 2, 13tc 1, 14c, 15tc, British Museum/Peter Hayman 18cla 21cra, 21c, 22crb, 22bl, 23tr, 23bc, 24bl, 26crb, 27tl, 27cra, 34tl, 34br, 35tl, 35ca, 35cb, 35br. **Corbis:** Carmen Redondo 24-25, Acetate 24, Acetate 25; Charles & Josette Lenars 11tl, 27bc; Gianni Dagli Orti 26cb, 26bl. **Philip Dowell:** Acetate 17. **Alistair Duncan:** 15tr. **Werner Forman Archive:** 14tc, 33cr; British Museum 22tc, 27tc; E Strouhal 34bl; Egyptian Museum, Cairo 19cla; Musees Royaux du Cinquantenaire, Brussels 37br. **Griffiths Institute:** The Griffith Institute Acetate 9 bl. **Robert Harding Picture Library:** Simon Harris 24, Acetate 24 bl. **Odds Farm Park:** Acetate 17. **Science & Society Picture Library:** Science Museum Acetate 16, Acetate 17. **Thames & Hudson Ltd:**

Hedi Grassley 24-25cb. **The Tutankhamun Exhibition:** Michael Ridley 30, Acetate 30.
Jacket credits:
AKG London: Egyptian Museum, Cairo back cover tc/spine, front cover. **British Museum:** back cover tl.
All other images: © Dorling Kindersley
For further information see:
www.dkimages.com

Every effort has been made to trace the copyright holders of photographs, and we apologize for any unavoidable omissions.
We have been unable to trace the copyright holders of P20 cla Scribes Recording the Harvest by Mrs Nina de Garis Davies (1881–1965), British Museum, London, and would be grateful to receive any information as to their identity.